Presenting:

RED, I SAID!

A SPREAD HIGHLIGHTING THE COLOR RED!

WORDS & ART BY: BRIANNA DAVIS

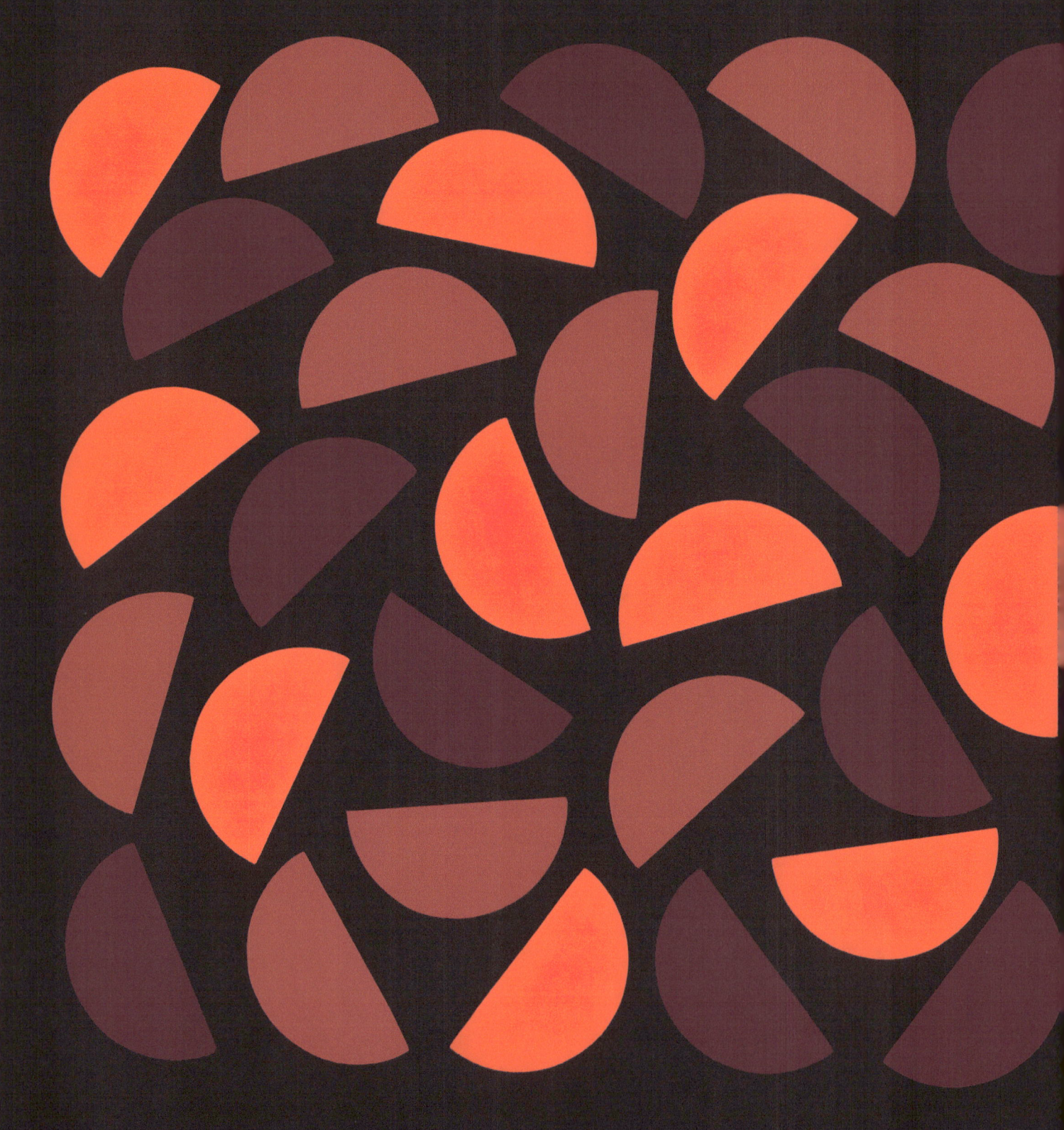

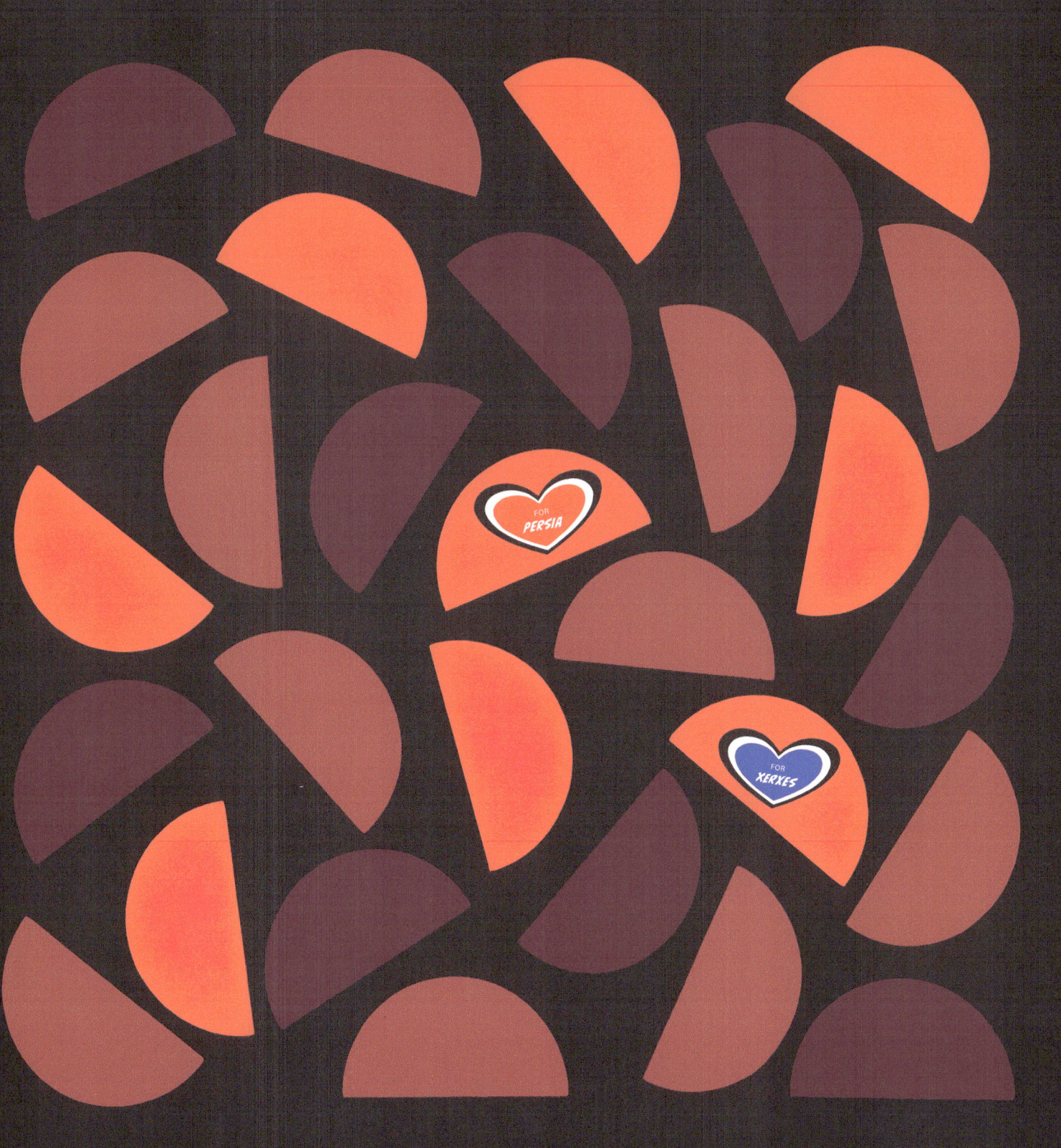

RED

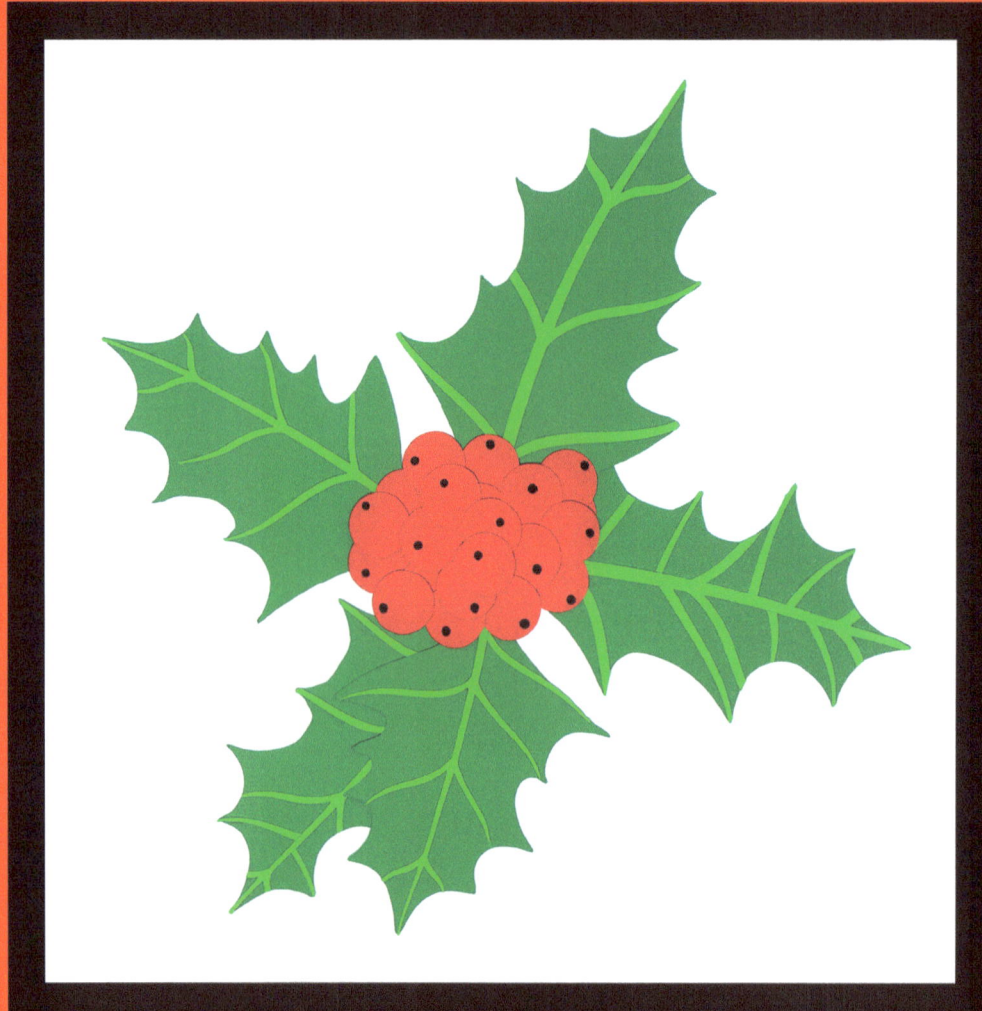

HOLLY BERRIES ARE A DECORATION FOR CHRISTMAS...

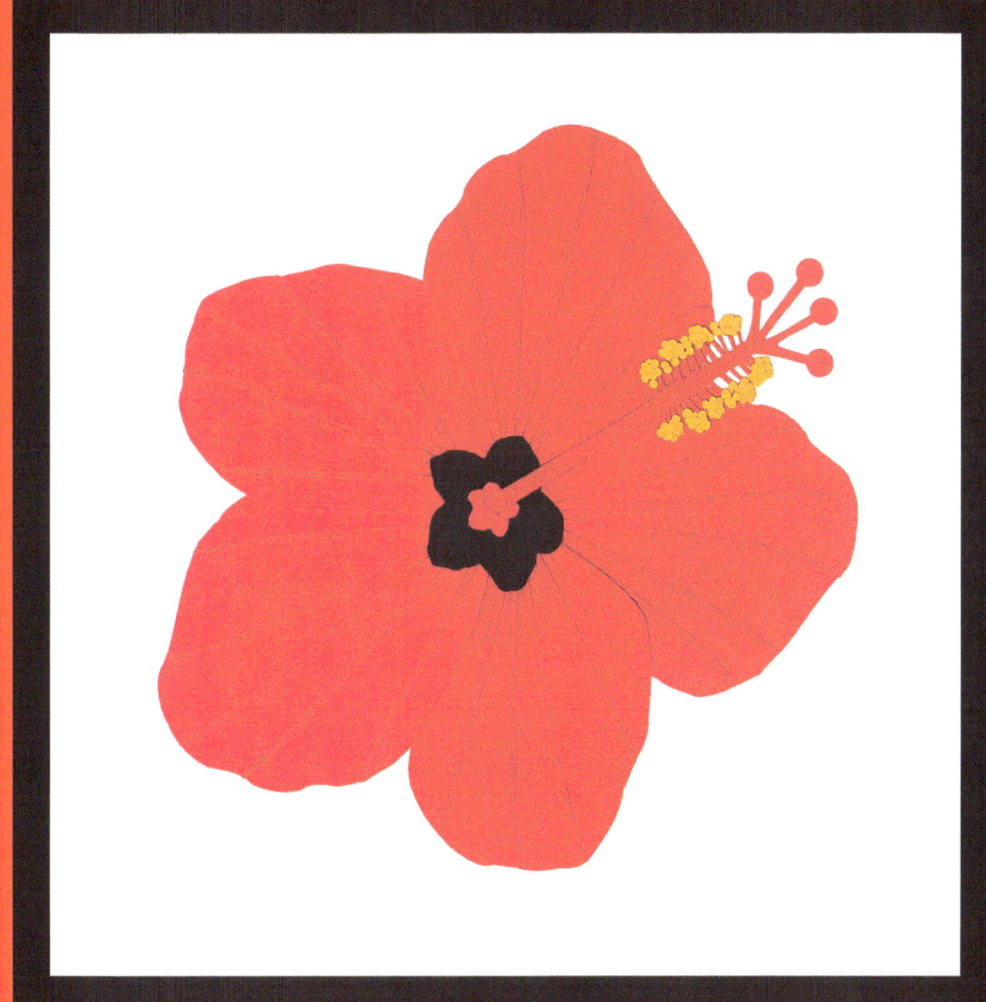

IF YOU'RE IN HAWAII, YOU WILL SEE THE HIBISCUS!

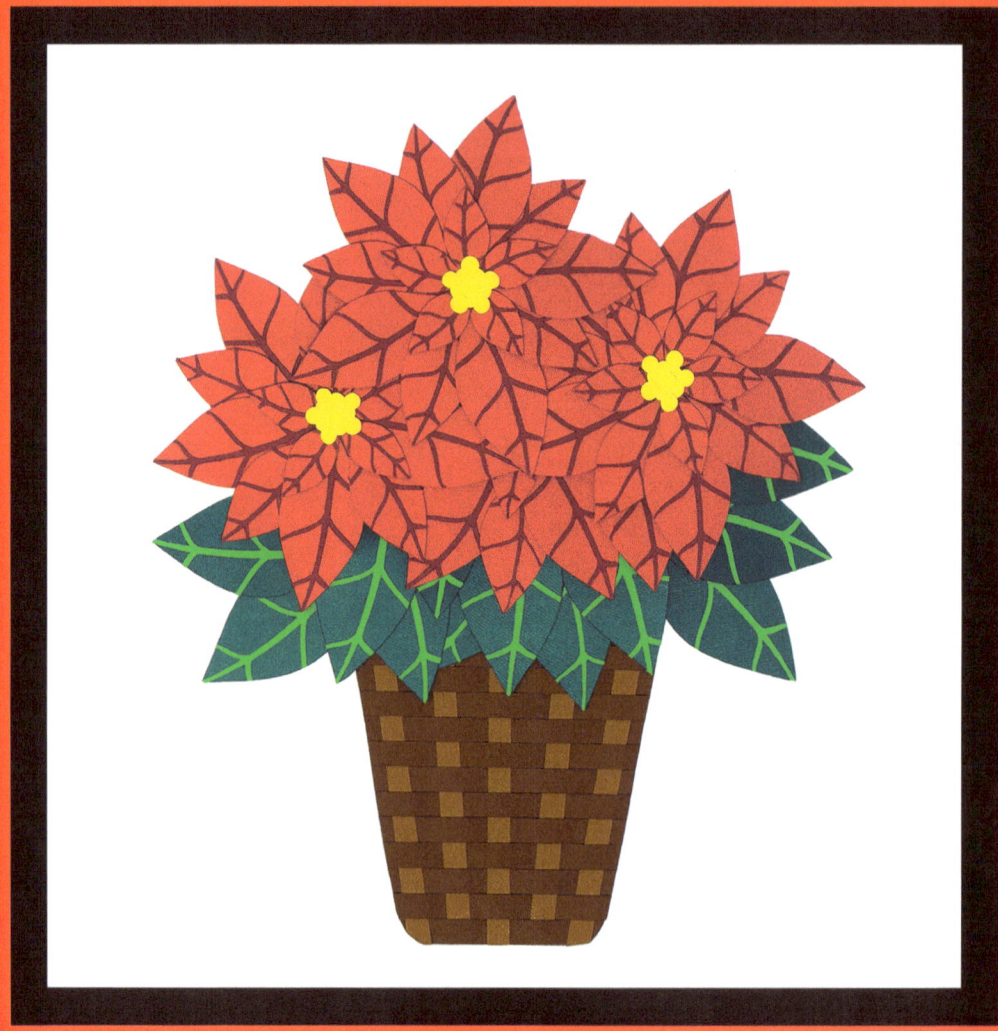

POINSETTIAS ARE KNOWN AS THE CHRISTMAS FLOWER...

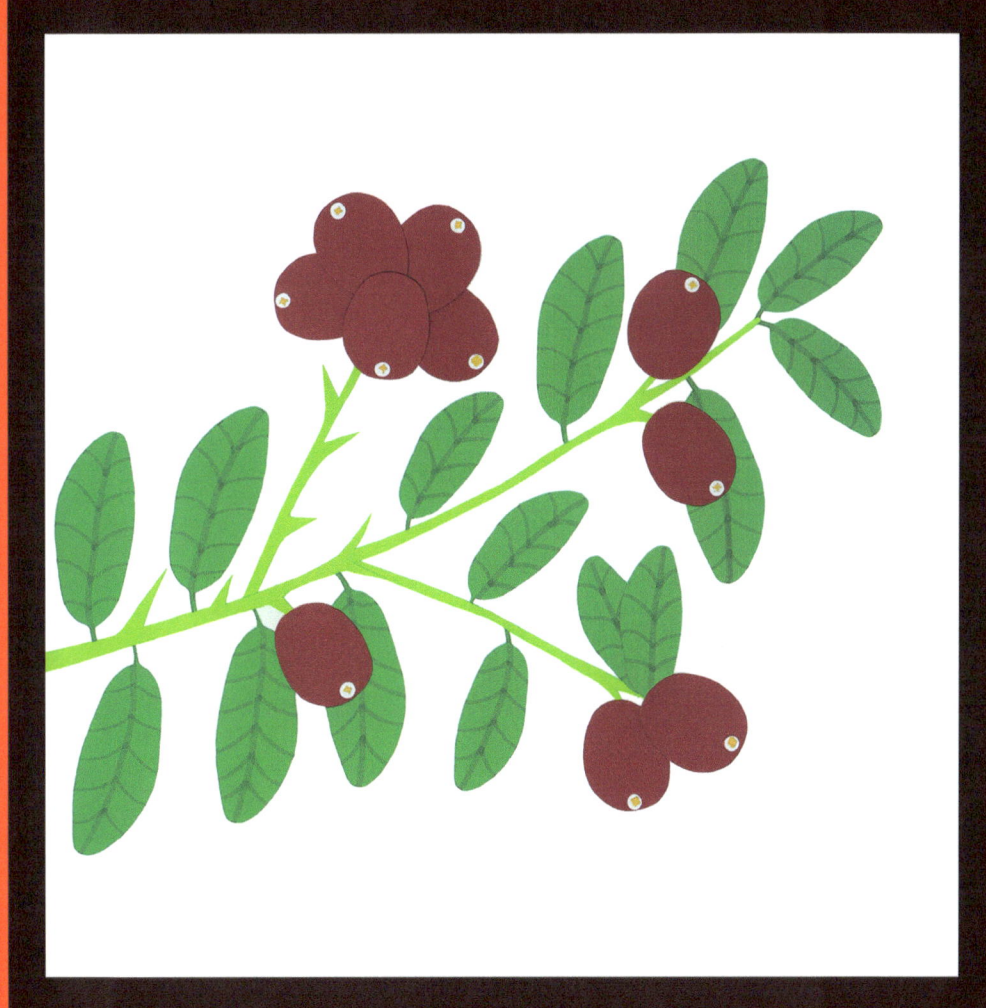

CRANBERRIES ARE VERY SOUR!

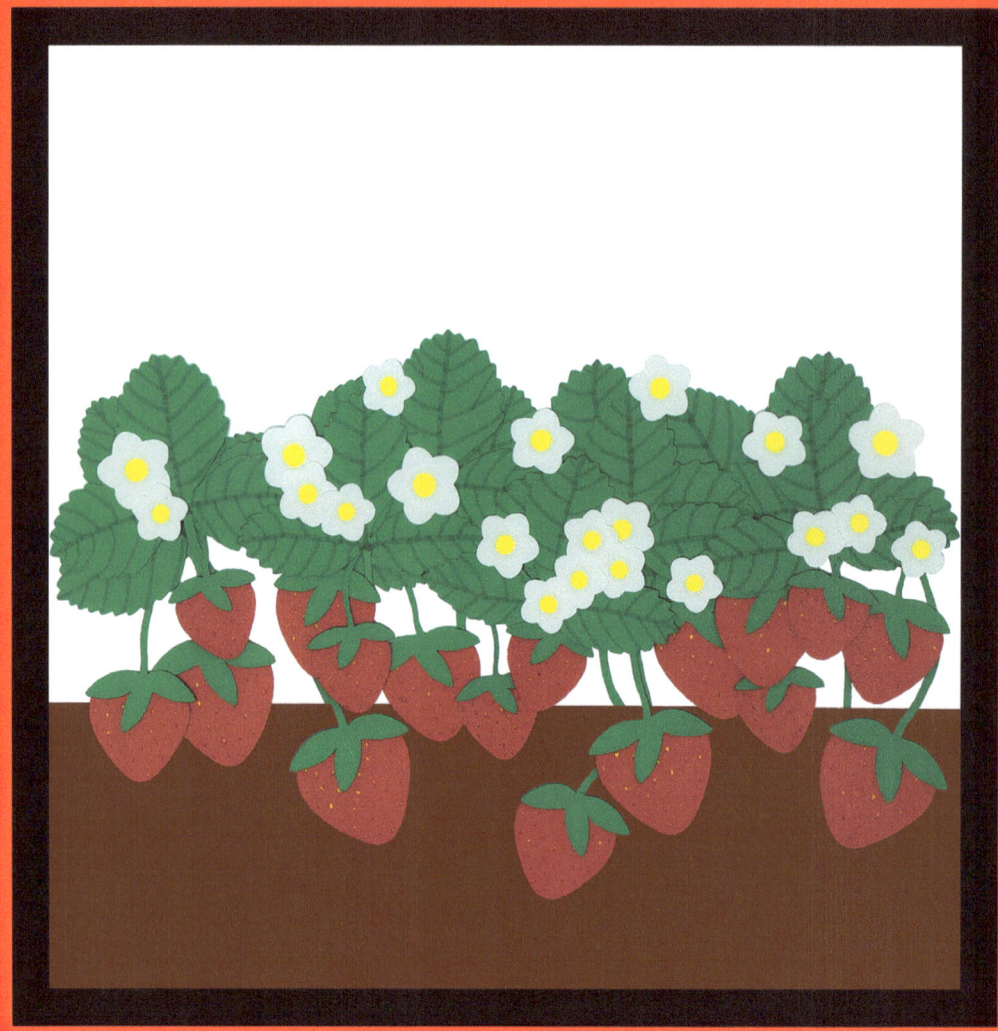

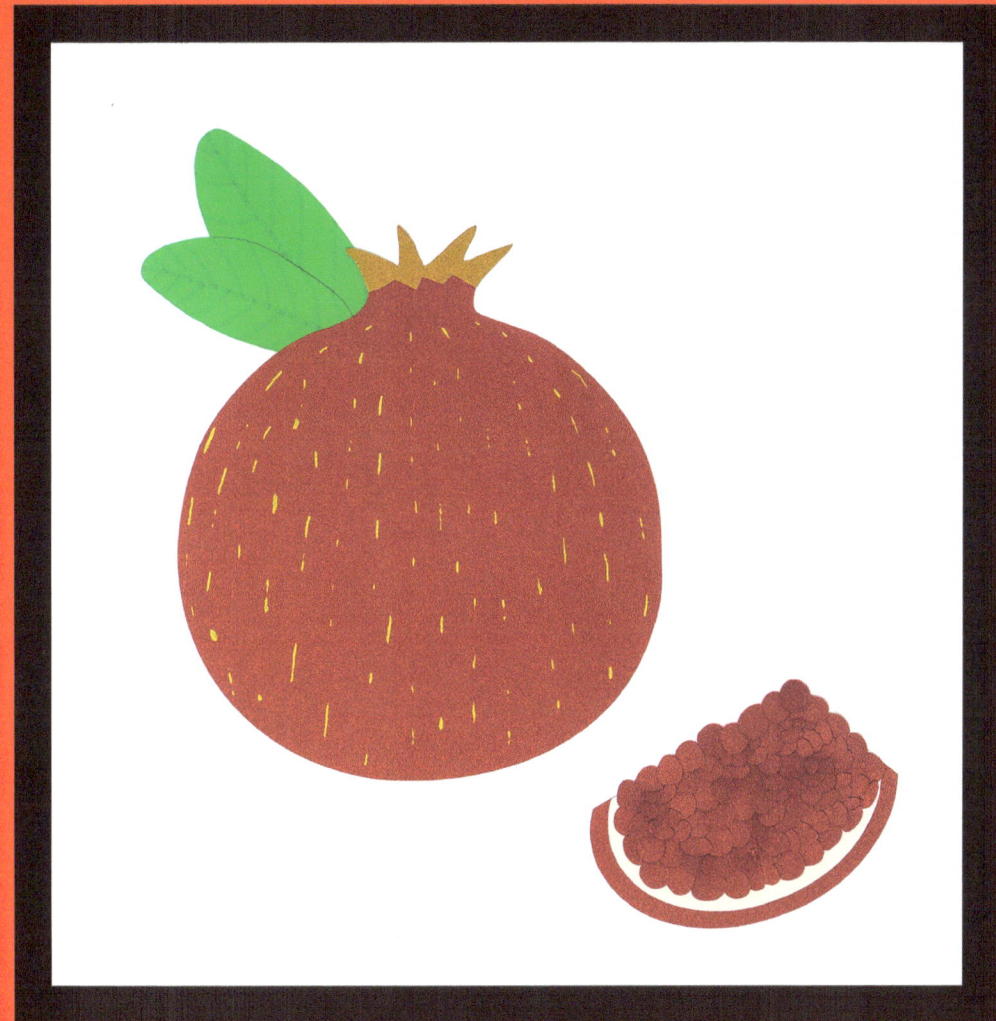

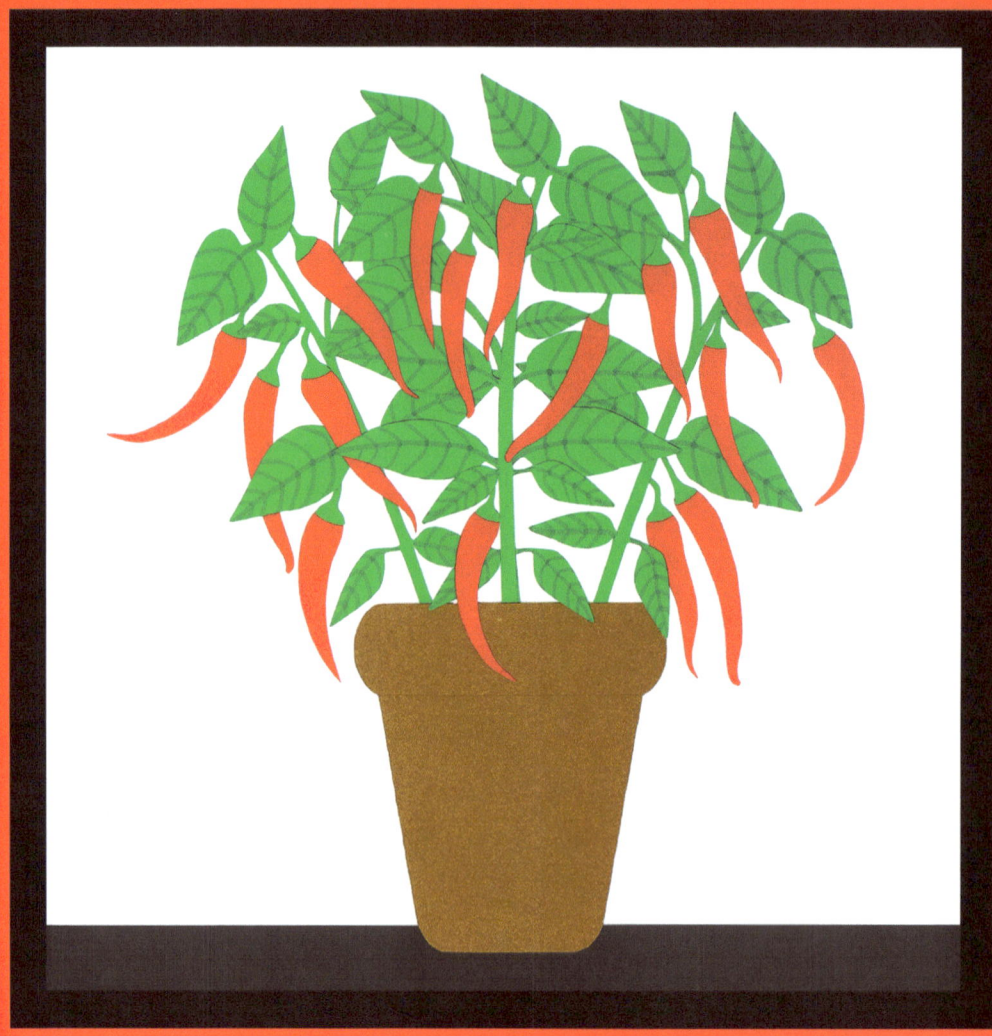

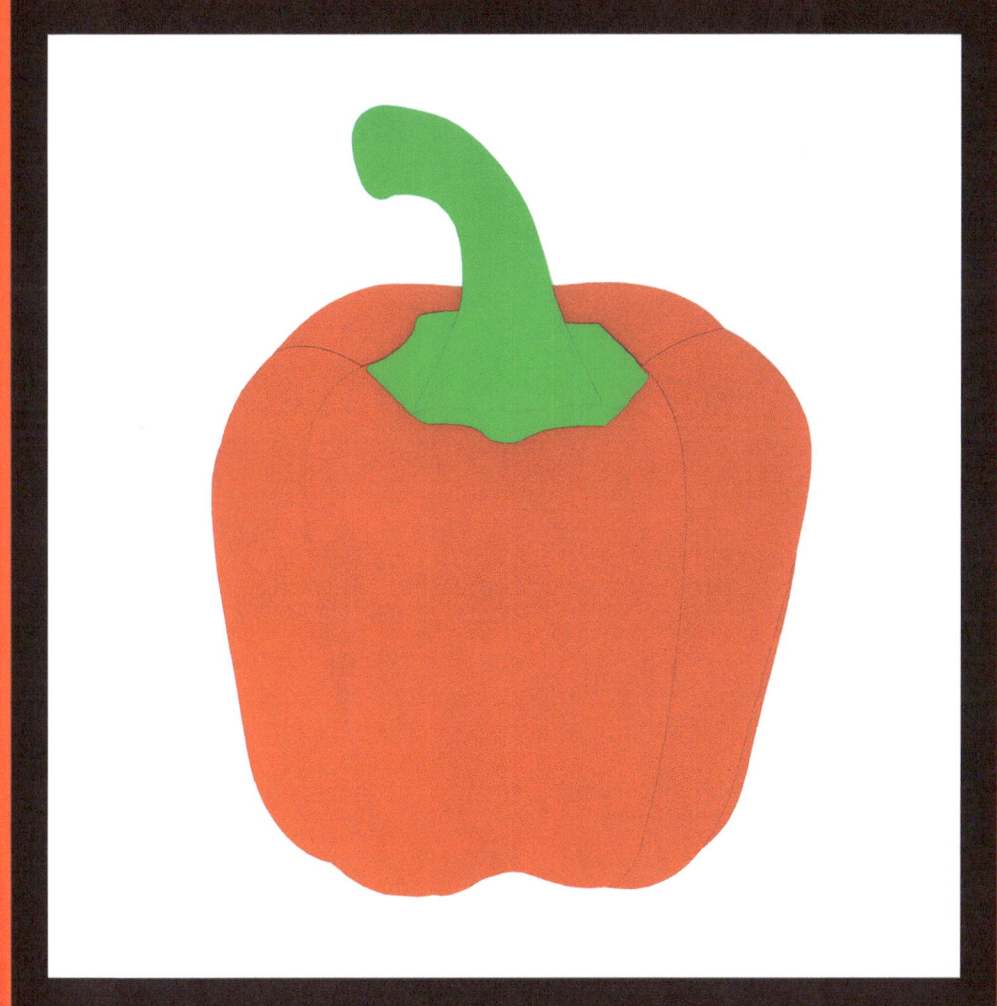

RED BELL PEPPERS ARE NOT!

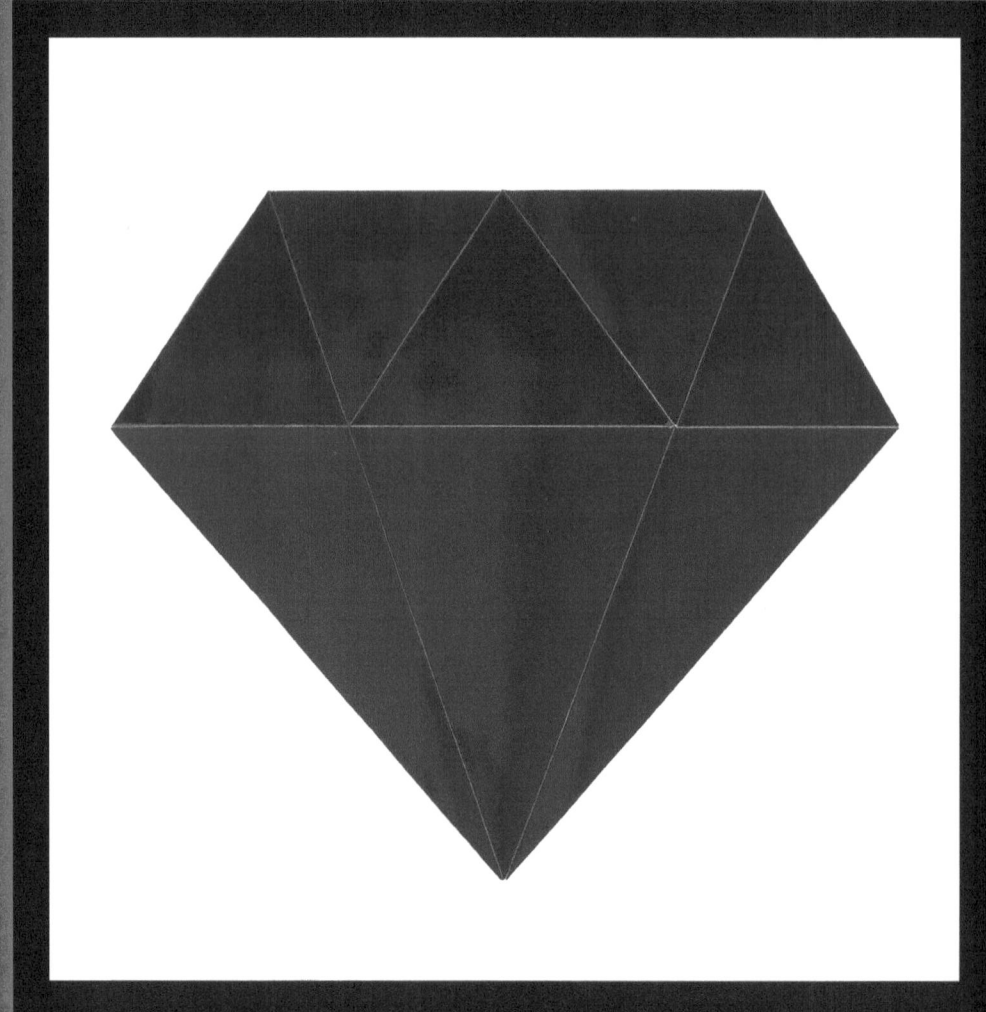

RUBIES ARE A DEEP RED GEM...

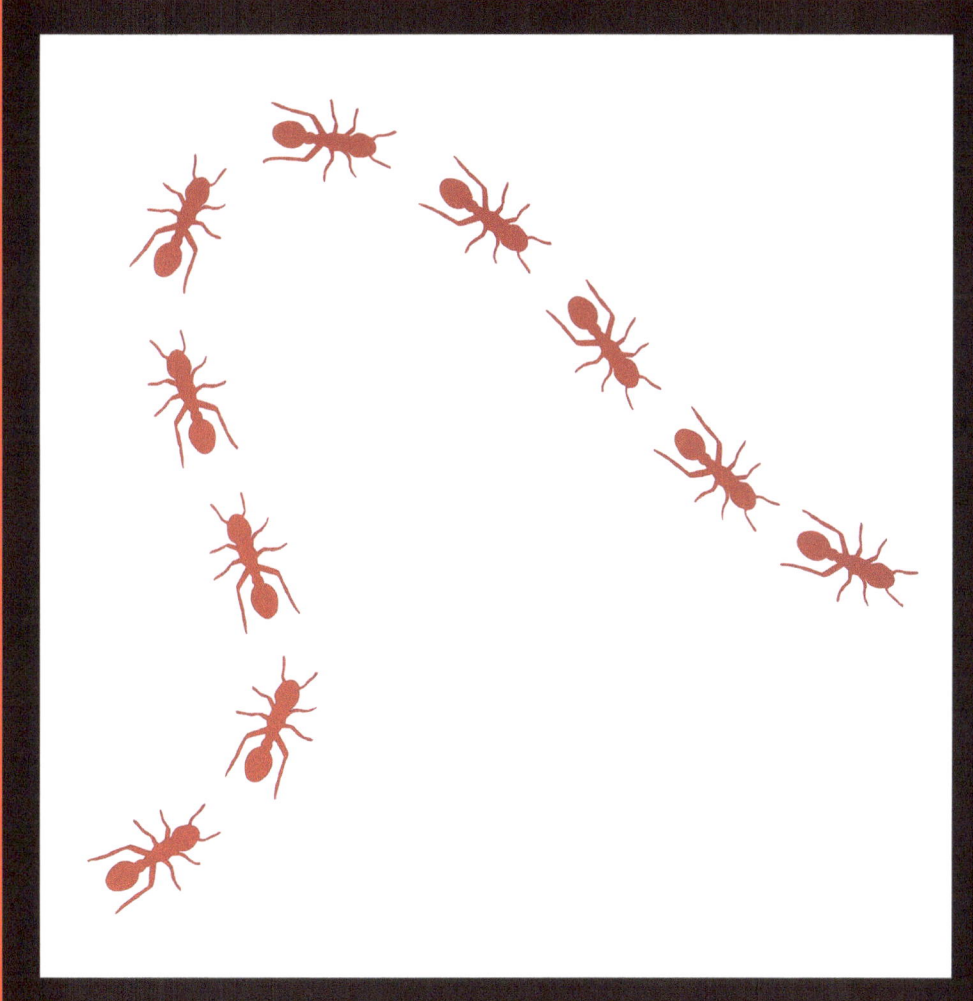

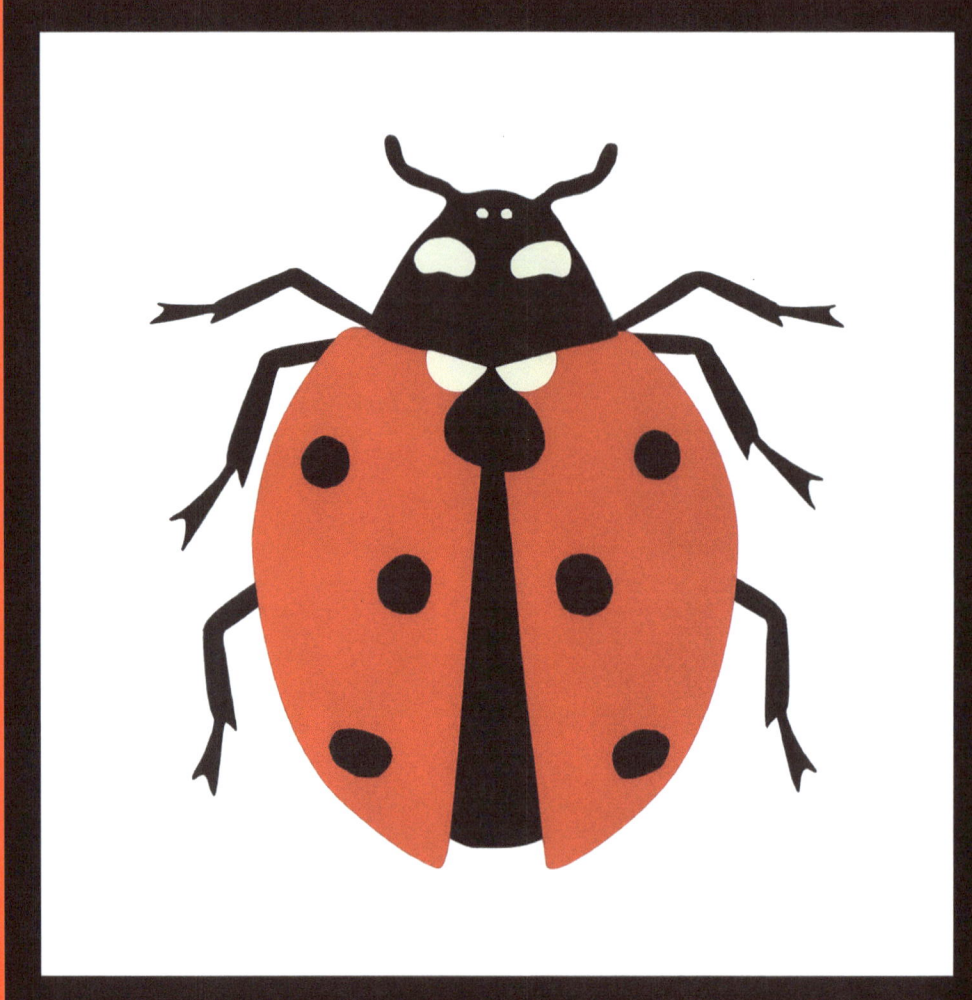

LADYBUGS ARE KNOWN FOR THEIR SPOTS...

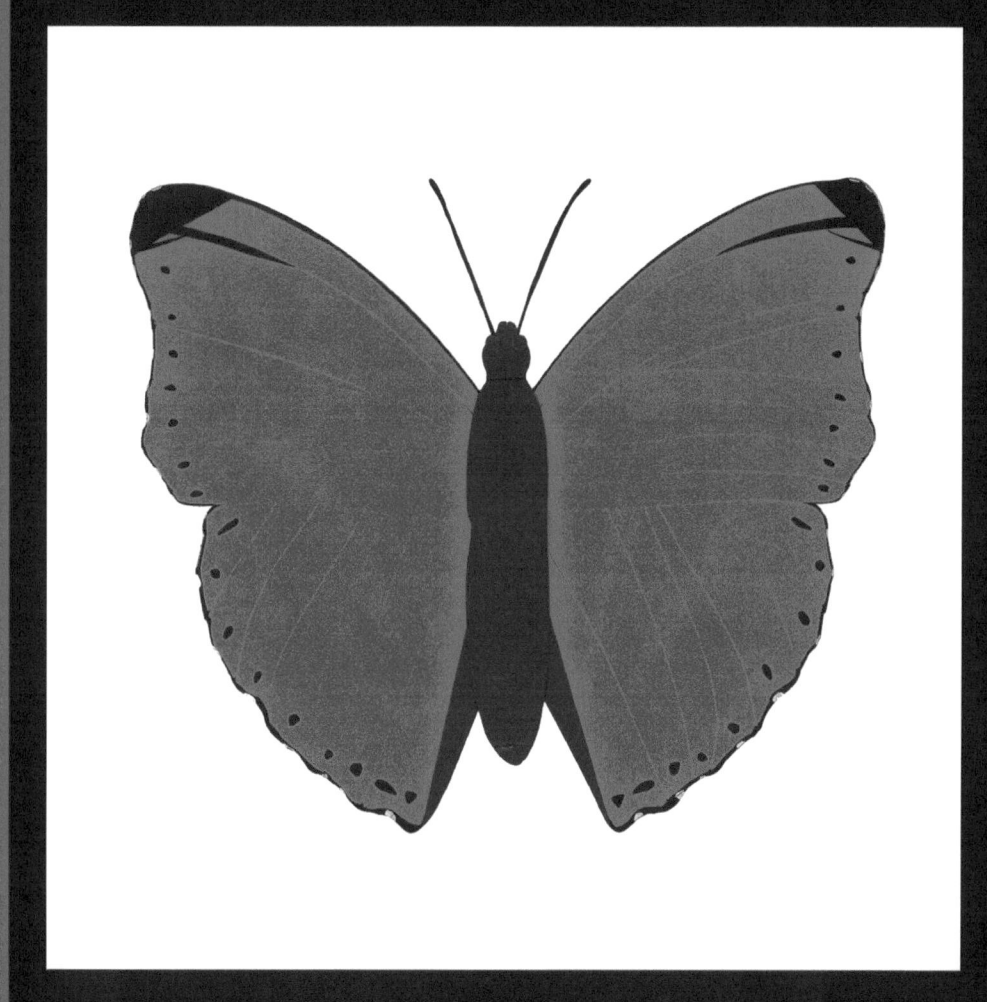

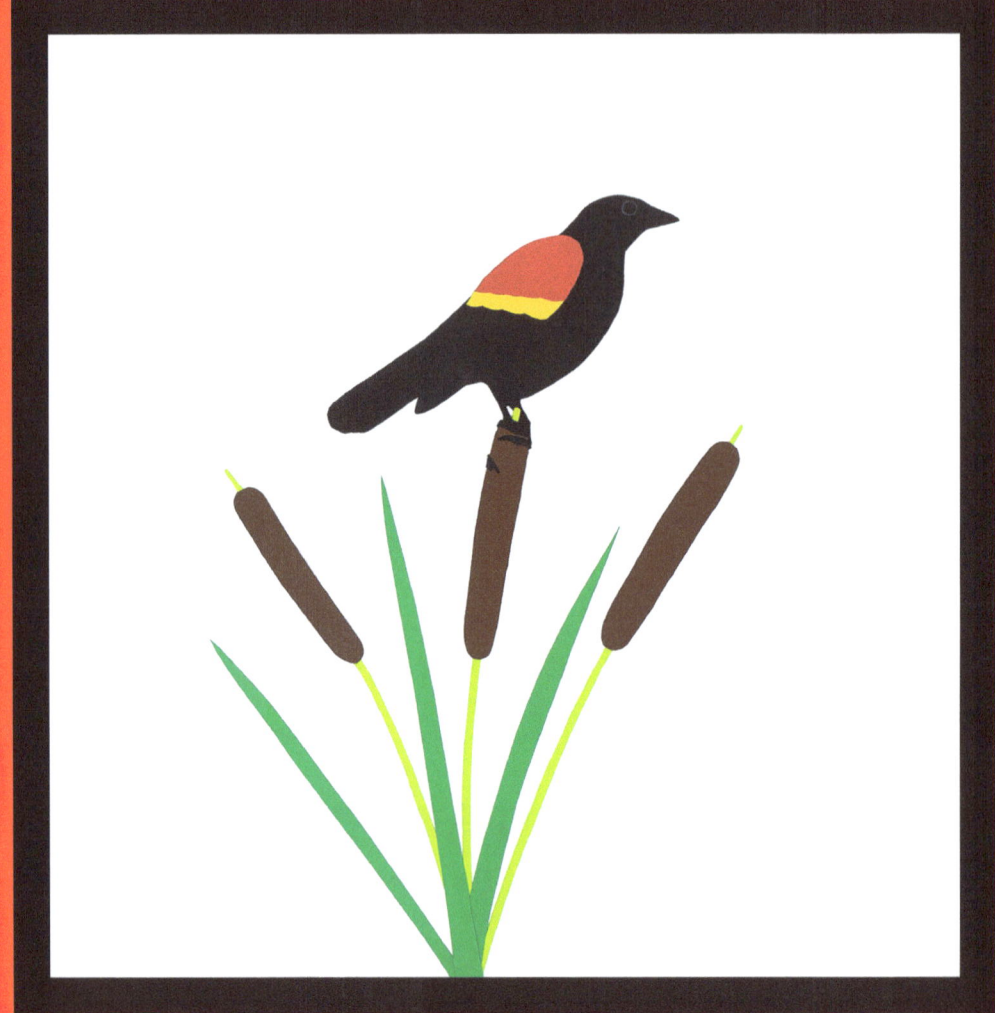

RED-WINGED BLACKBIRDS HAVE A RED SPLOTCH ON EACH WING...

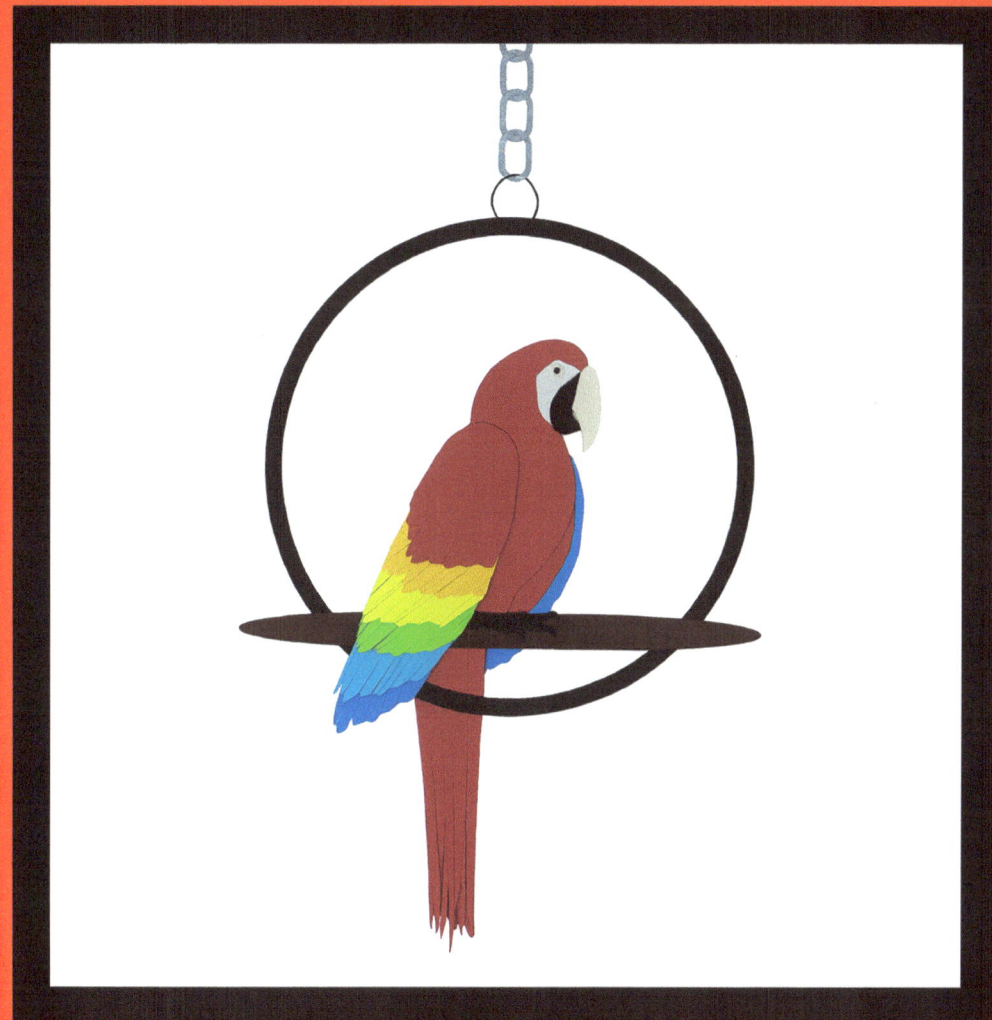

LOOK AT THE RED MACAW PERCHED ON ITS SWING!

LET'S RE-EXAMINE EVERYTHING IN THIS SPREAD THAT IS RED!

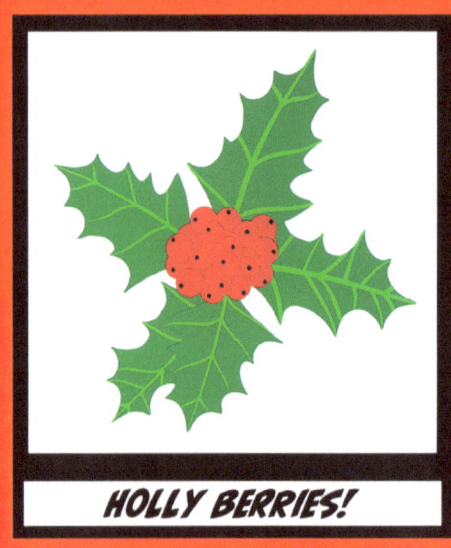

HOLLY BERRIES!

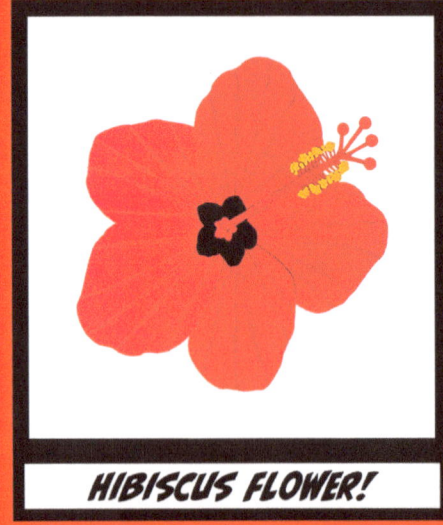

HIBISCUS FLOWER!

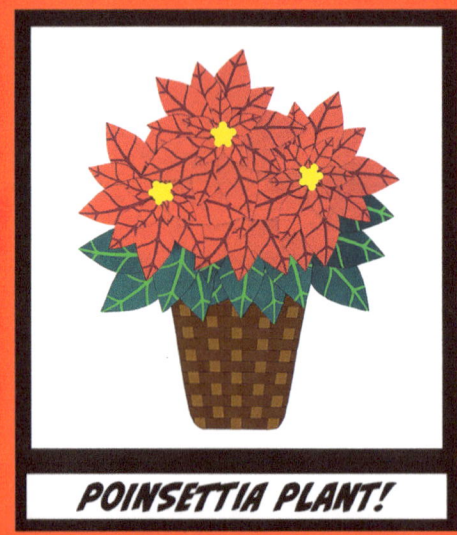

POINSETTIA PLANT!

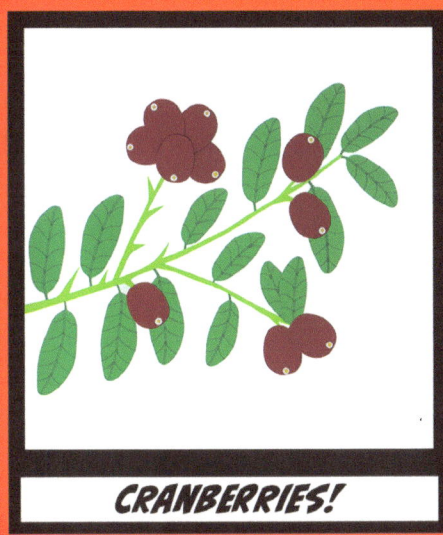
CRANBERRIES!

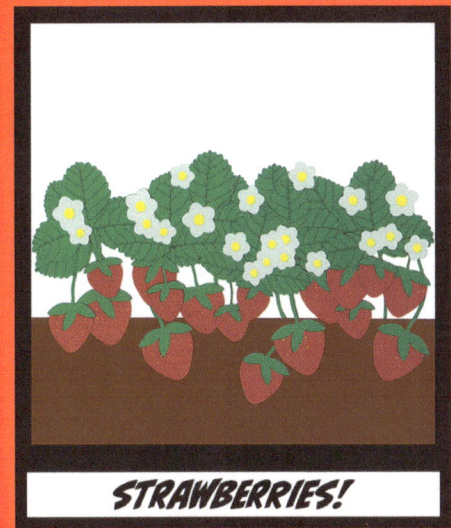
STRAWBERRIES!

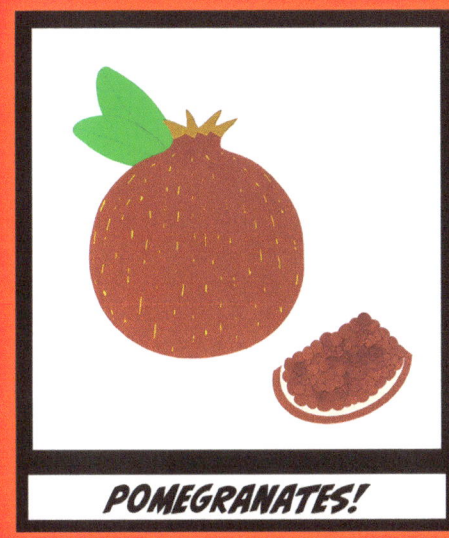
POMEGRANATES!

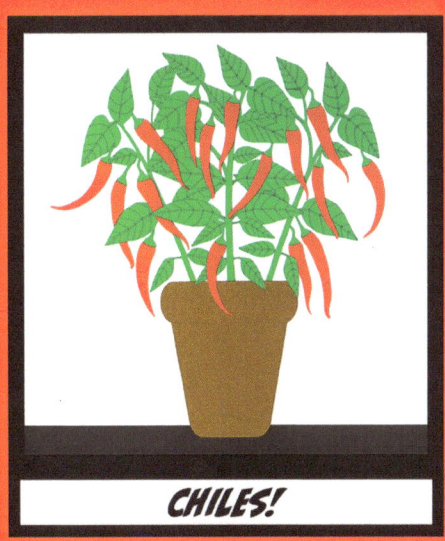
CHILES!

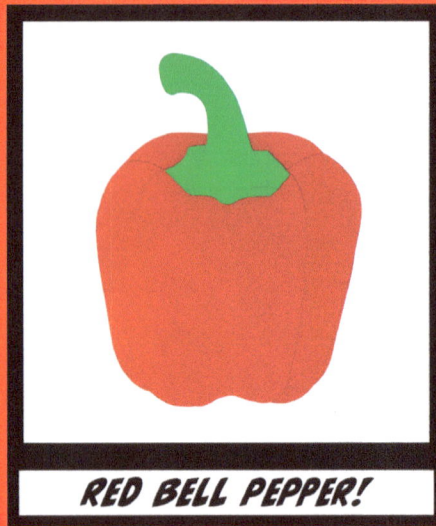
RED BELL PEPPER!

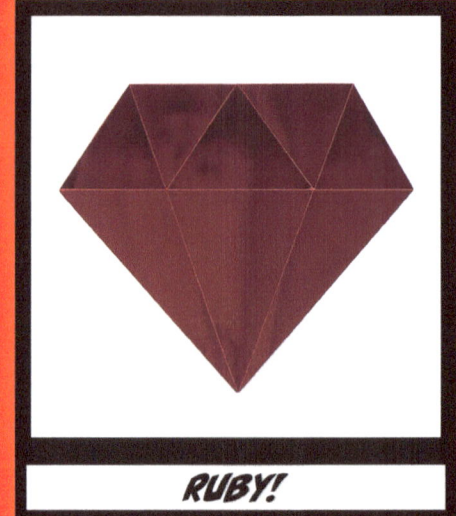
RUBY!

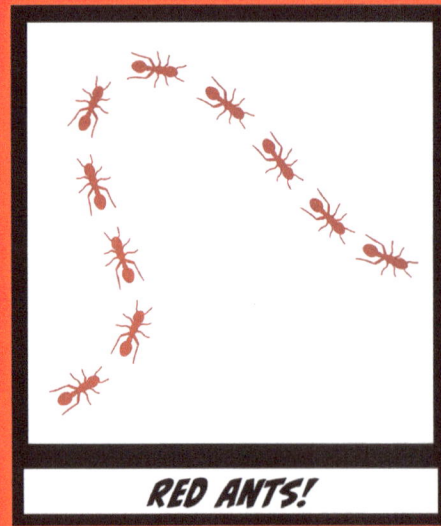
RED ANTS!

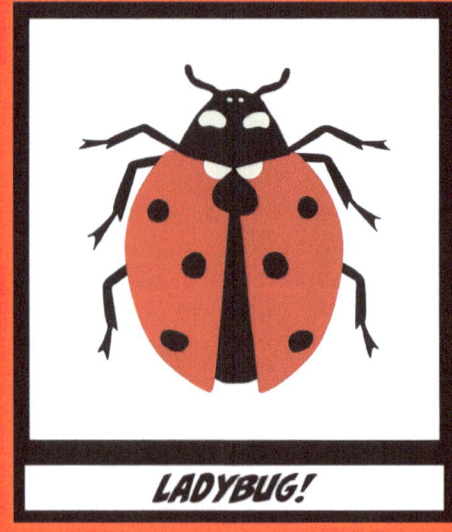
LADYBUG!

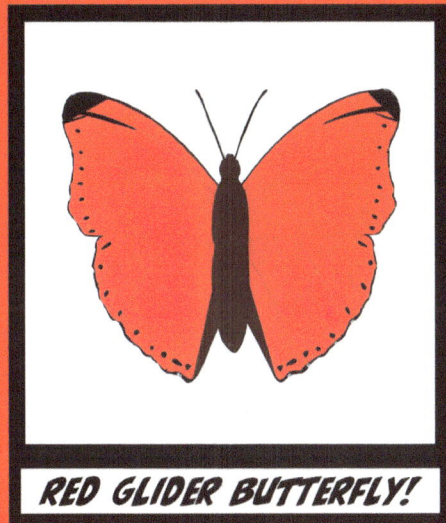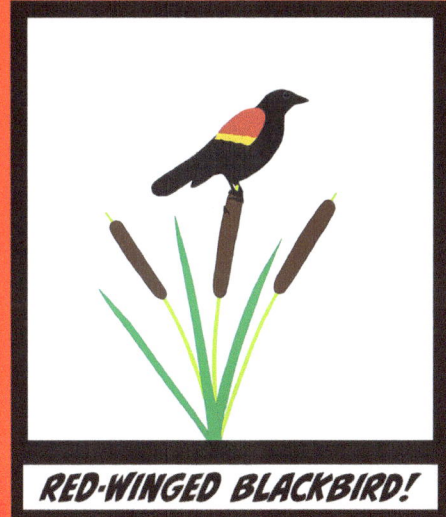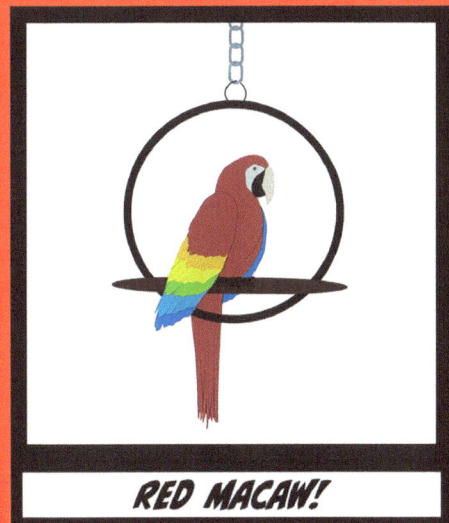

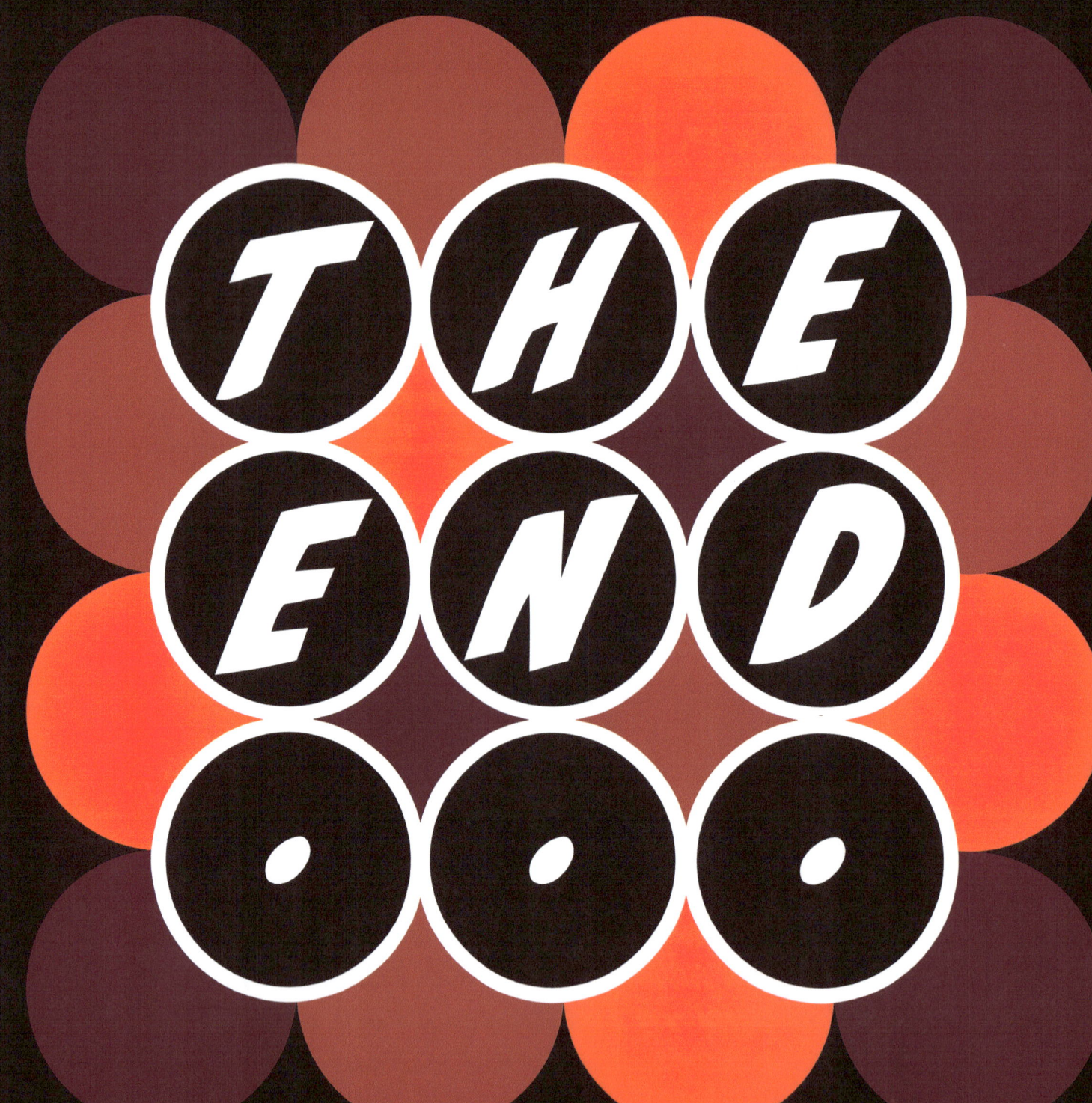

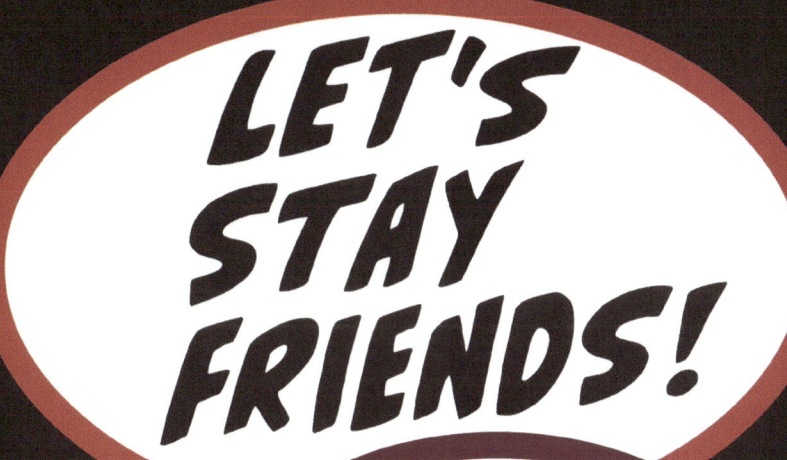

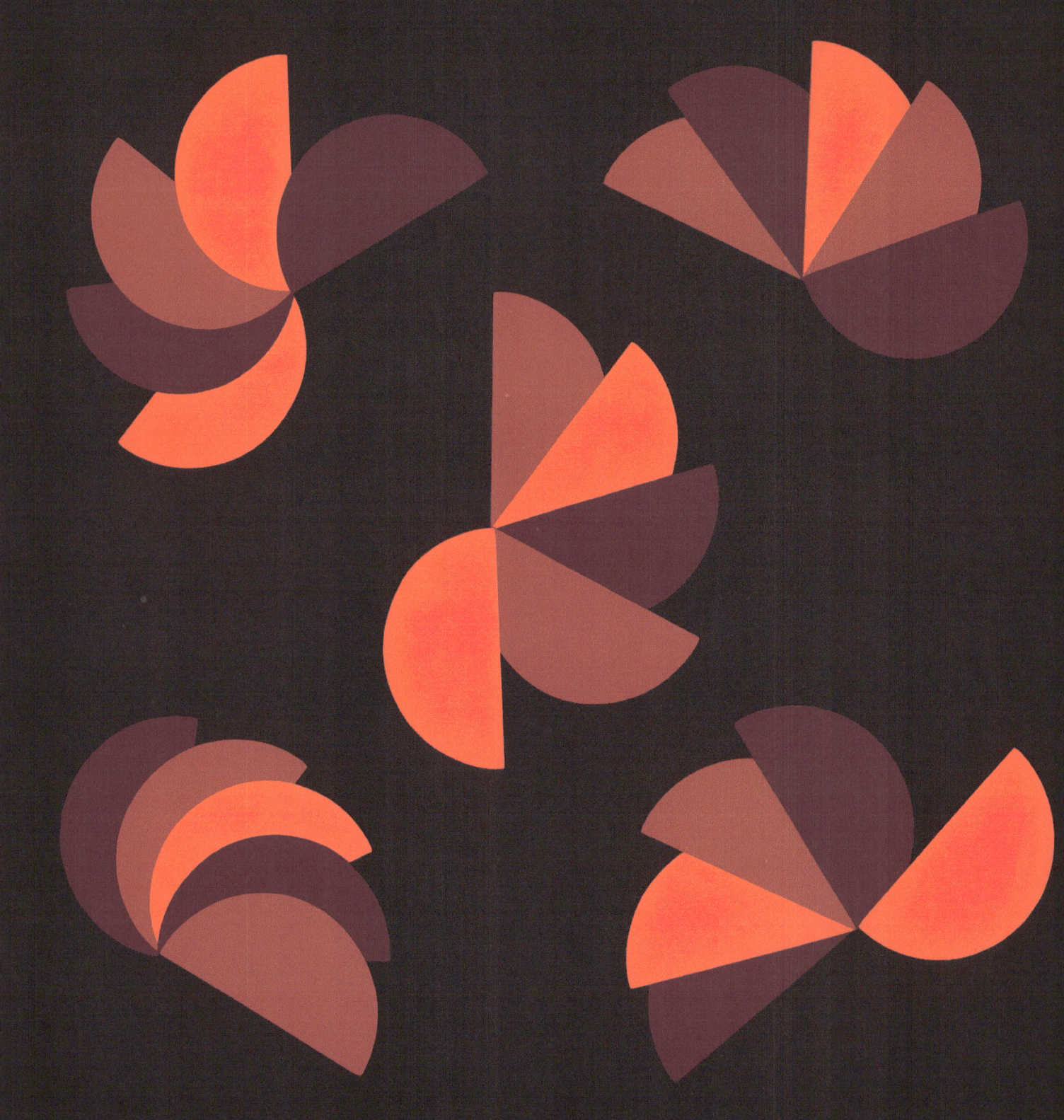

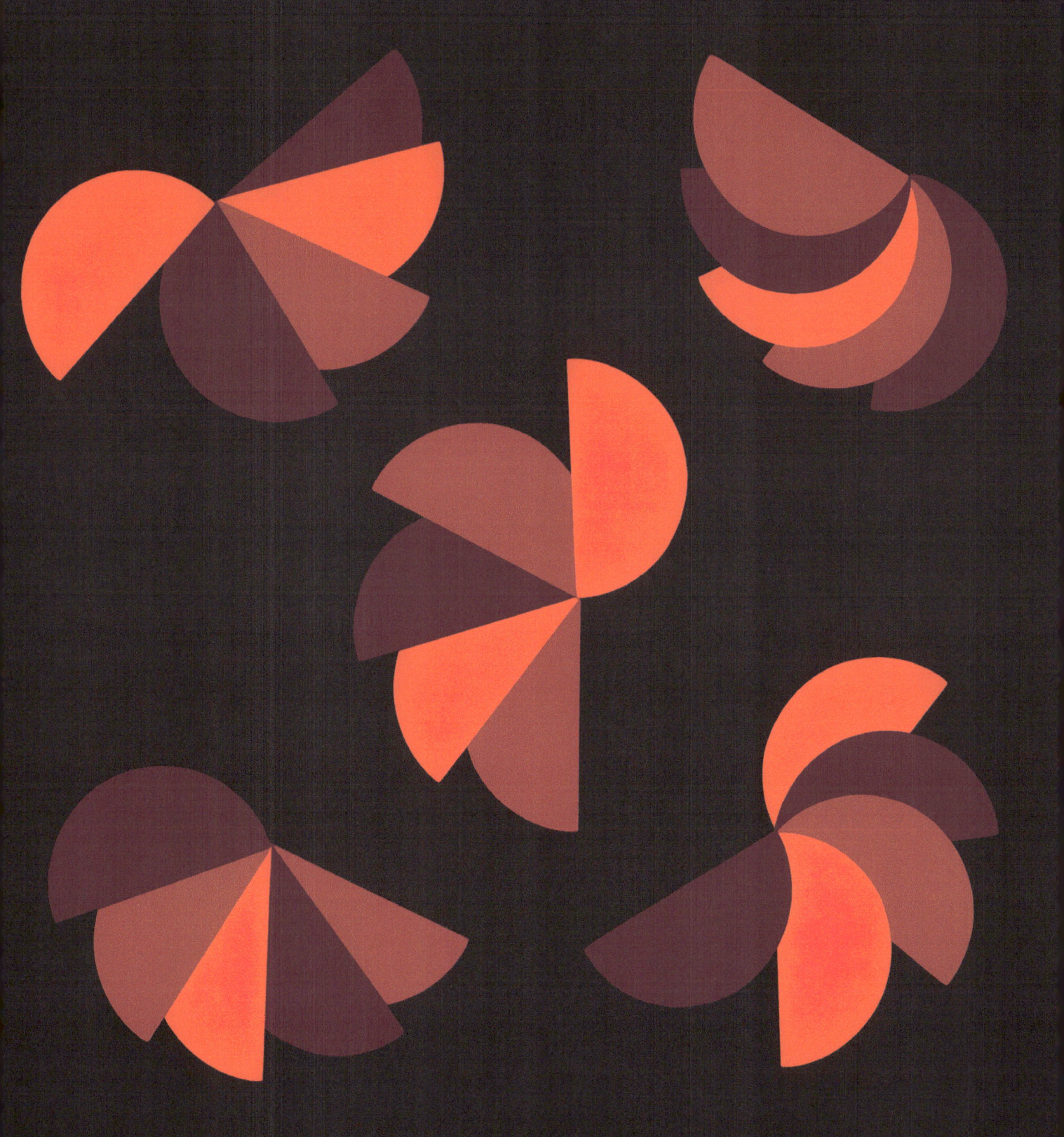

POP ART BOOKs AVAILABLE NOW

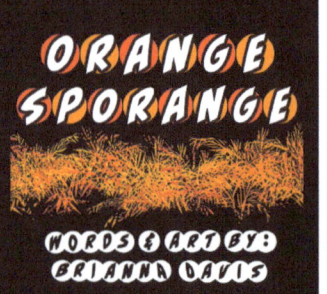
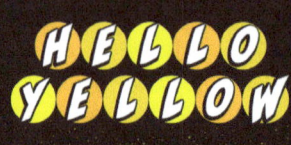
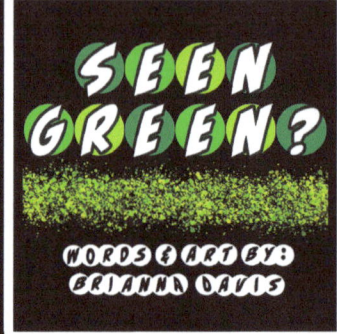
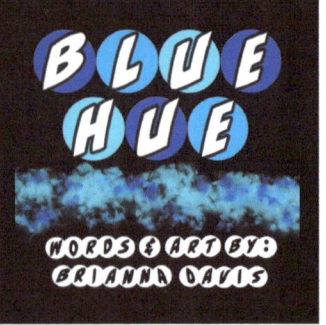
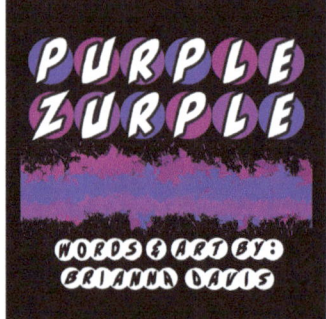
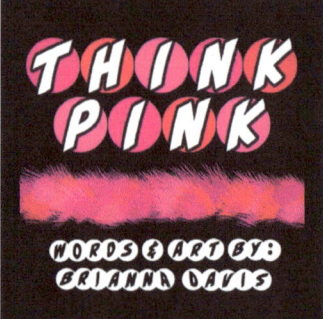
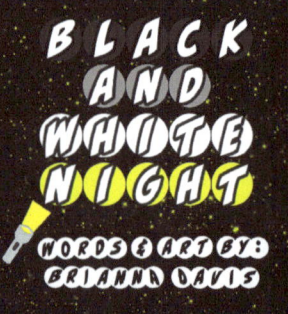
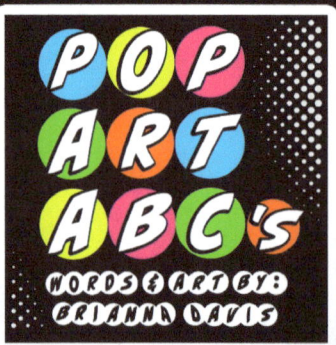
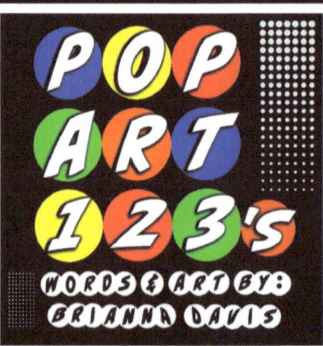

www.ingramcontent.com/pod-product-compliance
Lightning Source LLC
Chambersburg PA
CBHW051829210526
45473CB00005B/1801